C000095629

Taking control of your mind

Life hacks to resilience, confidence and success

WHY READERS
HIGHLY RECOMMEND
THIS BOOK;

"As soon as I'd finished this book, I wanted to get back to the beginning and start all over again. The way Mandie writes is so personal that it's like she is sat on your sofa, having a cuppa with you. The book is packed full of positive punches that will keep your mindset on track and gives practical ideas that you can easily incorporate in your daily life and business. I'm starting this book again with a Pen and paper to hand. I think I'm even putting one of your quotes on my wall!"

Helen Clyde, UW

Having just finished 'Taking Control of Your Mind' by Mandie Holgate I find that there are three things I must do straight away. 1. Book a coaching session with Mandie asap. 2. Buy her book 'Fight the Fear'. 3. Whilst waiting for those to happen, reread Taking Control and start working on it.

As an overthinker the insights are helpful, as a business owner they are invaluable

Paul Boorman, MCGB MCGC 'Focused Chef Ltd'

"The title of this book sums up everything I need to do in order to become more successful, and I know that so much of what holds me back is what my brain tells me (and no-one else!). The sections on "how to move forward when you're stuck in rut" and "calming those racing thoughts" were a great read for me, being someone who finds it hard to switch off and relax. Mandie has a fantastic straight-to-the-point attitude towards self confidence and makes you really look into yourself to find the issues and learn how to start with fixing them. This book is another must-read for anyone who feels they should be doing it all and every hour of the day, because you'll find the tools here to focus on what you really want."

Isobel Chaplin, MAAT IJC Finance Ltd

"Tips and tricks for every day. Fabulous read. Easy to pick up and read a little or a lot, depending on what time you have!"

Jenny Sjoellma, Pängels, www.pangels.co.uk

"My goodness this book is a tool box of gold dust. This book is a life compass that you can check in with 24/7 and remember that stars will shine in the darkness. Whatever your darkness I guarantee you will learn to have a healthy relationship with your mind and thus all areas of your life. Mandie is like gold dust full of magic, full of hope, full of empowerment and inspirational light. That is exactly what this book does, and I am exceptionally honoured privileged to have this gold dust in my life as my coach, but above all my friend."

Sheena Shanti, Spiritual Coach, wwwsheenashanti.co.uk

" I was so pleased to hear when Mandie announced she was bringing out another book - I'm addicted. As an independent business owner, having confidence and control of your mind and thoughts is so vitally important and reading Mandie's new book has given me just that - once you start, you won't want to put it down. Thank you Mandie, for always being so inspiring"
Alexandra Stanley Social Media Essex.

"I found it really interesting and thought provoking. Particularly getting me to think about what I really want and how I might achieve it.

I really like the straightforward style. I read the whole book in one sitting and I plan to re-read it with a pen and paper.

I liked that you discuss programmes and strategies fitting the person. It is so easy to think that there must be something wrong with you when a strategy does not work for you that seems to be working for other people."

Daliah Hopcroft, 42 Limited

Everyone's life experiences tough times, obstacles, and challenges.
In this book you will find the proven tools and techniques to overcome them all and it all starts in your head.

Learn how what you think impacts on what you do and the results you get.
Learn how to change the way you think to influence your resilience, confidence, and happiness.
Learn how to communicate in a powerful way to get what you want.
Learn the proven methods to achieving your goals, getting out of ruts and comfort zones, and getting what you want in every area of your life.

These easy to read and action life hacks could seriously change your life.

Each chapter features a most important mind issue and the strategies to fix it with case studies proving how these lifehacks work. Easy to follow short chunks ensure you can take it all in and take action.

When you've read this book, you will know how you were messing up your success and happiness and never let that happen again!

Mandie Holgate is a multi-award winning life and business coach and author of the highly acclaimed Fight the fear. Having coached thousands of people to achieve more there are more than a few millionaires who cite Mandie as the coach that helped them

achieve it and get what they wanted out of life.

Contents

FOREWORD BY CEO OF LIFEHACK, LEON HO

Everyone wants to lead a full and meaningful life with opportunities for happiness, growth, and success. We all have this need within us to be fulfilled, in every area of our life, to achieve a balance of pride and accomplishment--while still maintaining personal happiness through relationships and inner strength.

Yet, this is much easier said than done. Many people struggle with feeling inadequate, unsuccessful, and stuck. Perhaps you had big dreams and goals, but as the years have gone by you've seen these fade into oblivion. Or maybe you've simply lost your post-college enthusiasm and can't find any way to get back on track.

It doesn't have to be this way. The secret of overcoming your obstacles starts in your mind. If the thoughts that run through your head are causing you stress and dissatisfaction, your outlook on life is likely to be gloomy and pessimistic, and you may struggle to reach your goals. Conversely, if you learn to hone your thoughts and mindset towards success and opportunity, you'll have a much easier time reaching your goals.

Of course, unpleasantness and obstacles will happen; they are part of everyone's lives. Honing your mindset towards progress and opportunity means that you approach unpleasantness in a more positive and productive way. Instead of taking everything as if you're a victim of negative circumstances, you see challenges and obstacles as an opportunity to learn and grow.

Deciding on a goal is relatively easy. But it's also very easy to give up on a goal when the going gets tough. These can be goals like making big career plans or moving to a new city. At first, these goals probably seemed straightforward and achievable. But perhaps you encountered difficulties (which is inevitable and part of life), and your desire to complete the goals took a hit — and eventually you gave up on them altogether.

If this sounds like you, you're certainly not alone. Everyone feels like giving up at some point, especially when it comes to setting and meeting goals. We face obstacles. They slow us down. And sometimes they can bring us to a complete stop. But that doesn't mean you shouldn't keep going...

As someone who has been working within the life improvement sphere for the past 15 years, I was honoured to be included in this book. Lifehack.org is a website I started in 2005 as a way to share "life hacks" that I had discovered in my own quest for self improvement. Since then, Lifehack has grown into one of the most read self-improvement websites in the world, attracting millions of monthly readers. We are proud to have over 30,000 articles on self-improvement published at Lifehack.

...and we owe a huge part of that to our dedicated and talented writers, which Mandie Holgate is among.

At Lifehack pride ourselves on offering the very best self-improvement articles and advice. Our courses offered through Lifehack Academy teach you how to reach success, no matter where you find yourself in life.

We also believe that mindset is incredibly important when it comes to improving one's self--in fact, we believe that it is an essential first step. What's wonderful about this book is that its entire premise is based on this notion and is fully expanded upon to give not only an overview, but a practical guide on how to implement this in your own life.

Mandie has compressed a wealth of exceptional information from her own professional experience so that it is easily digestible and beneficial for those looking to expand and improve their own potential. She introduces a relatable framework and provides solid advice on how to find your own archetype and make the most of it towards personal success in your own life. Within this book is a clear-cut guide to help you better understand your own patterns, so you can understand the power of harnessing your mental strength.

The beauty of harnessing your mental strength is that it creates a positive snowball effect that will transform all areas of your life, as well as enabling you to have the confidence to create the life you've always dreamed of. It teaches you how to tap into your potential so you can confidently set bigger and brighter goals to enhance your life.

Presented in an easy to follow format, this book will enable anyone struggling in life to become better versions of themselves. It outlines techniques and extremely useful tools that you can integrate immediately to start living a better life, no matter what your current circumstances. It's a straightforward guide for those wanting to lead a successful and satisfying life gleaned through the author's experience coaching others. It teaches you to listen at the right times to and trust yourself to accomplish what you set out to do.

This book truly is an excellent resource to have in your arsenal to help you build resilience, gain confidence, and reach success on your own terms. And when it comes to personal fulfilment, there is no better time to get started than right now.

I wish you all the best in setting these tactics outlined in this book into motion. Cheers to you on your journey to self-betterment!

Leon Ho
CEO and Founder of Lifehack

CAN A BOOK HAVE 2 FOREWORDS?

When I wrote this book, I wrote to some of the amazing people I am lucky enough to know to see if they would write something for the front of the book. Imagine how honoured I felt when 2 international giants of mindset and success replied and wrote so many amazing things about this book! So as Gordon and I discussed it our belief about what is acceptable to put in a book is created by our beliefs, so why not? Over to you Gordon...

"Belief is the number one influence on whether you will be successful or not, that's is a fact.

Now that doesn't mean that just because you believe you will be successful that success is guaranteed, it doesn't. But it does mean that if you have doubts about your ability, or that you don't think you will be successful then this will become a self-fulfilling prophesy and failure is the likely outcome.

When you believe that you will be successful, and things start to go wrong you will spring into solution mode, looking to see what went wrong and what you can do to turn it around. Whereas if you don't have the belief, when things start to go wrong you go into, *I knew this would happen mode*, and you will stand by and watch as things go from bad to worse.

If that lack of belief is strong enough, then you probably won't even bother to start.

Our brains are so powerful, and when we have doubts, we set our brains off looking for reasons not to start, and more often than not we will find them and quit before we even start. When you can control your mindset then you can have more control over the outcomes and have a higher chance of achieving your full potential.

I've written over 1500 articles, three books and have had nearly 200 articles featured in publications such as Forbes, Inc, Entrepreneur, Fortune, Chicago Times, Fox News, Additcted2Success and had my work translated into 21 different languages. My last book FAST was a finalist Chartered Management Book of the year. All this was achieved by someone who knew for sure he couldn't write and had nothing to say that anyone would want to read.

If only Mandie had written this book 20 years ago, I would have been able to see through the lies I was telling myself, I would have been able to ignore the fears that were holding me back and start down the path to achieving my true potential.

In this book Mandie gives you simple, easy to use and easy to follow strategies that you can use to get over yourself and put yourself in control of your potential.

We all have that little voice inside our heads that tells us we are not good enough, that we will never be successful, and that maybe we should save ourselves some pain, and not even bother to start. This book will help you quieten that voice and replace it with Mandie's positive, encouraging voice that will help you take those first steps on your journey towards success.

With her background in coaching we know that her approaches are tried and tested. I know that with her coaching and guidance she has helped me shake some of the other beliefs that have held me back, and I really appreciate her infectious enthusiasm which literally jumps off the page.

Thanks Mandie for this great guide which I know I will read many times and will keep coming back to for guidance."

Gordon Tredgold, Global Guru's Top 10 Leadership Expert & Speaker

WHAT'S THIS BOOK GOING TO DO FOR YOU?

Have you noticed how some people seem to get what they want, and others seem to work just as hard (if not harder) and don't get there?

That has always fascinated and infuriated me in equal measures.

It seems really unfair and while I know life is not often fair wouldn't it be good if you could level the playing field a bit?

Having coached thousands of people and mentored and motivated a good few thousand on top I know what stops some people from getting what they want in life and rarely is it access to funds, new skills, new jobs or degrees.

It all starts in your head.

So, if that's the case, would it be great to hear you can do something about it?

Whether you want to wow a boss.

Take over the business world.

Buy your dream house.

Start something new.

Stand up for what you believe in.

Stop getting bullied into looking after everyone else and never getting what you want this book could help you achieve that and a lot more.

As a coach for many years I have seen people from the age of 13 to the age of 78 utilise coaching with me to get what they want (and get rid of what they don't want). It's an amazing process to be able to help people understand what is going on in their heads and how it is impacting on their success.

In this book we take some of the top techniques I've used with my clients from CEO's and students, from business leaders to international speakers, from corporate teams to classrooms to help them understand how their minds are impacting on the results they get.

I have coached people in sometimes what has seemed impossible situations and they are still in contact with me many years later because our time together was so life changing.

I really hope this book does the same for you too.

You can just read this book cover to cover, head straight to the chapter that resonates with you the most or you can have a pen and paper to hand so that as you work on each chapter you can take notes and really start to build a picture of what is going on in your head.

In this way it is like the process I go through with my coaching clients. And with every client I take copious amounts of notes that allow us to see where they were and how they move forward. It makes for fascinating and enlightening reading as you move forward to help you stay motivated.

Don't dismiss how powerful this book could be to every aspect of your life.

Remember it is your mind and no one else's that matters as you read this and if you find you struggle to understand how you would use a tool or strategy from this book you really are welcome to get in touch via social media. I'd love to hear from you.

All social media links are available via www.mandieholgate.co.uk

Good luck and keep in touch.

6 TYPE OF FEAR AND HOW TO FIX THEM.

Like many things that stand in the way of you achieving what you want, rarely is it the thing you think it is. That's really annoying because you can't fight a demon you can't see.

In this chapter, I want to share with you 6 archetypes that you might not recognize that actually come from your fear of success.

They're stealthy, sneaky things and rarely that obvious but wow they can damage your success or even your perception of it, and worse of all, many are playing out automatically in your life already!

For each Archetype, I want to share:

- The signs that this archetype is attacking your success.
- Things they say (Not you, you've no control – at the moment over this.)
- A strategy to overcome this attacker on your success.
- Good news about your hidden archetype
- A success story so you can see how it works (and doesn't work!)

1. THE GOAL ADDICT – TYPE 1

If you are a goal addict, you are not averse to setting goals. You achieve big. You know what you want and go for it.

The Goal Addict Type 1 can be an overachiever. There's nothing wrong with wanting massive levels of success. However, when they sit before me, they are not working with me to become more successful. They want to find ways to relinquish control, or slow down.

They desperately want to escape elements of their life; or they notice how un-fulfilled they feel despite the healthy bank balance, awesome looking life style and illusion of the perfect life.

The Goal Addict T1 is likely to say:

- I decided to get fit and now I am.
- I achieve what I set out to achieve – no excuses.
- I hustle until I get what I want.
- I'm keen to tell you I achieve big.
- There's no time in my life to watch TV/read a book/do nothing.
- I just hit our quarter targets 5 weeks early.

Strategies to Employ

Whether it's you that's the Goal Addict or someone you love or work with. Giving them some space to talk and explore who they are is not likely to work.

They achieve big because of who they are and they can't see any reason to change, so don't try to enforce change on them or yourself. Instead, find out what the Goal Addict doesn't like about their life.

You will need to choose your timing well. If they feel threatened or cornered, they will be quick to let you know how awesomely successful they are.

When you find yourself berating something in your life, don't shut the thought down, explore it and ask yourself:

"What does this mean to me?"

"How is this impacting on my happiness? Health? Loved ones?"

Don't choose the normal parameters that you'd normally choose to work like "What does this mean to my work/financial freedom/success? You will quickly prove yourself right and won't deal with what's going on.

The Good News

The good news about Goal Addicts is that they really appreciate their skills, attributes and successes. They can stay motivated and on track no matter what happens. They have an inbuilt determination and tenacity that helps them achieve big.

Working Towards Success!

I've worked with many incredibly successful people who have told me they are not happy. They've been on a permanent drive to get to the top they never stopped long enough to check the destination was still where they wanted to get.

One client realized they were trapped on a hamster wheel and we went back to basics. This quickly enabled them to see that 20 years of striving to be the best had been great but it had been costly. They had no one they felt they could love, no social life and hadn't been on a plane for pleasure in years. Taking the step back and reacquainting with who they really are, helped them appreciate that the person they'd been years ago still existed and they reconnected with that.

They now do a lot of travelling. They still work as hard, but the weekends are as important as the day job.

2. THE GOAL ADDICT – TYPE 2

The Goal Addict Type 2 is possibly the opposite to the Type 1.

They still achieve everything they set out to achieve, however, they achieve small. They aim small, keep it small, and achieve small. And then when they talk to their coach, boss, friend, or loved one, they are complaining that they aren't getting what they want in life.

They can be frustrated and disappointed and are less likely to shout about what they achieve, want or need.

The Goal Addict T2 is likely to say:

- I never seem to get where I want to go.
- I find it really hard to visualise the future.
- I wouldn't know how to tell them.

Strategies to Employ

Goal Addict T2 often present to me with a sense that they could achieve more but aren't. They tell me they lack confidence or that they don't want to rock the boat. They like things fair for all.

The issue with this approach is they aren't keen to explore what they really want. (It can make them hyperventilate and anxious to consider big goals and big ideas.)

Make use of the science of being you. Start by understanding that you have the skills, beliefs and attributes to achieve. You've been doing it for years. It's just your focus has been up too close. Don't try and process how you will achieve big or even what you want to achieve. Just notice how you've got as far as you have.

Know that failure is good for you. While many of us have heard this, The Goal Addict T2 is petrified of it. It links to lots of fears and while it may manifest as the fear of success, often underling this are the fears of what people will think of me and the fear that I will look stupid. Most fears at their base have the fear of what other people will be thinking about you.

So, before you look to overcome your fear of success, build your confidence. In my experience, the quickest ways to build your confidence is 2 fold:

Get a really clear focus on what you want out of life (tough for the Goal Addict Type 2 right?

So work with someone to help you work out what that looks like.

Remind yourself of your genius and skills. They already exist you just don't want to look at them. And a word of caution – if you find your confidence levels are impacted on by what is going on, then that's external confidence and it's doing you no favours. Learn to build your internal confidence.

No one gets out of life without making mistakes. We learn far more from failure than we do from success. Search online and you will find tons of articles talking about some of our great achievers in every arena of life – and so many will tell you that it was their failures that enabled them to be successful.

Failure is not failure, it's the chance to learn.

The Good News

The good news is that Goal Addict T2 are good at motivating others because they'd rather look at other people than them-selves.

Also because they don't know where they want to go, they are easy to be with, manipulate, employ and control. (Okay you can see that can be bad for the Goal Addict, right?)

They are good at protecting themselves from failure and negativ-ity because they just won't look at it in that way.

Working Towards Success!

I worked with someone who told me that they had no proof that they could achieve anything. Everything they'd ever achieved had been because someone else had told them to do it. They didn't create the spark; the small flame was handed to them.

By using the strategies above, they rocketed their confidence, learnt to trust in what they had to say, stop stressing about what other people were thinking of them or of what they said and learnt to push themselves.

Some people like to get so far out of their comfort zone they can't see it any more. For this person, it was about small goals that added up to the big goal – something they obviously knew they could do!

3. DISBELIEVERS

The disbeliever is less likely to come to me for coaching of their own free will. They are more likely to be a member of a team and the senior team has spotted some issues that they feel coaching can help overcome.

The disbeliever has a fear of success that is manifesting itself when they fight change in the work place or can justify why things can't change.

They say:

- We don't do it like that.
- It can't be done.
- That would never work.
- That's outside of my skills.
- Strategies to Employ

Be aware of the language you use on yourself. Does it empower you or undermine you? You may think that your language is keeping you safe.

Imagine for a moment that the very thing that you felt kept you safe was in actual fact keeping you trapped? Becoming more aware of the trap that your language creates, enables you to get out of it faster.

Don't go it alone. If you are fearful of success and hold strong beliefs about what can't be done or what you can't do, it's going to be tough to fight that alone.

Challenge what you believe. Your perception of reality is unique to you. Only you have reached this place in exactly the way you have, so be mindful of how that journey has skewed your view of the world.

When someone challenges you on what you think can be done, don't' be so quick to dismiss them. Take some time to process it – could this be the way for you to fight your fear of success?

The Good News

Disbelievers hold strong opinions and those opinions have kept them safe. (Yes, you could reframe it and say those ideas have kept them trapped) but for now, know that they are good at holding strong in their views.

Disbelievers also tend to be sticklers for doing things the right way. (Yes, they can get bogged down and fearful of trying new ways) but for now remember they are good at being really reliable and sustainable in what they do.

Working Towards Success!

I was working with a team that had 2 Disbelievers in. The rest of the team were pretty much despondent that they'd ever get on board with new ideas and new ways of working. So no matter how much new methods were enforced on the team, the disbelievers could always justify why the old way was best.

We made it very personal to them, and talked about how the new ideas made them feel. How they felt unappreciated and like they were considered the "old dogs" of the team that couldn't learn new tricks. They could, they just couldn't see the benefits. "It had all been tried before."

We stopped talking about their beliefs around the changes, and looked at what they hated about their roles at work. Then, we looked at ways to make things better. The team were able to show the Disbelievers that the new ways of working would in actual fact deal with the very issues they faced.

The Disbelievers were so trapped in their view of reality there was no space in their beliefs and automatic processes that would enable them to access the new ideas. This process enabled them to do it and helped the team see the challenges it caused for the Disbelievers.

A greater understanding of each other led to some serious eureka moments for the whole team. That means happier staff and less stress as well as increased productivity!

4. SABOTEURS

The Saboteur thinks they are doing their best. They work long hours (they aren't afraid of hard work!) they go for it, they try new things but it never seems to work out the way they really would like it to.

No matter what they do, they never feel like they've good enough or done enough. It's a constant fight.

They say:

- I will do all I can.
- I can't see how this is going to work, but I will do my best.
- This is not my area of expertise so I don't think I can do this.

Strategies to Employ

The Saboteurs have it tough because no matter what happens – good or bad, they can find something to be unhappy with. Even if things are going great, they will be able to tell you the things that went badly.

Head and heart is an exercise where I get the Saboteur to just talk about something they aren't happy with, something they feel can't be achieved. They can talk in depth about everything that went wrong, can't be done, and has been considered and dismissed. However, ask them to list out everything they learned or benefited from in that experience, they struggle.

Persevere because the Saboteur is good at finding what is going on. And with help, they can force themselves into looking at what exists — really exists. Head is the facts that they know (the easy bit) and heart is the stuff that they choose to think (the tough bit).

Step back from the situation that you fear and get the head and the heart to create the dialogue. Even if you don't believe it, the facts can start to shout louder than the feelings.

The Good News

Saboteurs should celebrate how hard working you are. You get knocked down again and again and still you resiliently get up and go for it again!

Working Towards Success!

The Saboteurs' fear of failure can make them a bunny in head lights, trapped and unable to move.

I've seen the head and heart strategy work powerfully, because you can't argue with the facts (as much as you may try) slowly, this process enables the person to take a new approach, create new beliefs and even achieve more.

One client would every month sit before me and tell me why something wasn't good enough and how they'd failed. Until at one session, they sat before me and said my own words back at me "I know, I've achieved a lot and I wasn't achieving this much 5 months ago, was I? So I don't even have evidence to that fact, do I!"

This made them laugh because clearly, they were getting their own new message loud and clear – and I love working with that person!

5. THE HALF HEARTERS

Of all the fears of success, the Half Hearters are least likely to work with a coach. I meet a lot of these in my line of business. They are often following me around the UK to hear me speak or reading every word I write online but still, they ask the same questions and are doing the same things. And we all know that's a definition of madness, don't we?

Half Hearters are usually sponges at taking on new information and can repeat it back parrot fashion, but they don't actually take action on it.

They are likely to say:

- I saw your video and thought it was very interesting.
- I did that, and it didn't work.
- I don't think that strategy could work for me.

Strategies to Employ

With some fears, you need to look at it firmly in the eyes and deal with it head on; others are fought by concentrating on what you really want and eventually the fear shrinks to nothing because you build your confidence in what you do.

For Half Hearters, they are convinced that they have tried everything and are doing everything they can. It means that no matter what they learn, they don't take action because the underlining fear has control — subconscious control, but control none the less.

Then, try the "And that means" exercise.

When you find yourself saying something ask yourself "And that means?" Keep asking this question.

As a coach. we get to work deep down in your mind finding out what the route issue is. This process helps you do that too. For instance:

"I don't think that strategy could work for me."

And that means?

"That I will have to accept that I can't do that in my life/business/career/relationships."

And that means?

"That it will always be a limitation on my success and happiness."

And that means?

"That I will always fear this."

This process helps you see what's happening to you because you won't attempt something new.

Now use the "If I knew, what could I do" exercise. For this, suspend reality for a moment. Get the magic wand out. Get creative. There's no limitation on your time, health, finances, abilities, skills or beliefs – with that in mind how would you answer the first statement again?

And yes, I know for many, this is way out of your comfort zone, but the least creative clients are able to find some insight too. So stick with it.

For instance:

"I don't think that strategy could work for me."

If I knew, what could I do?

"If I knew it would work, I could do it."

This then enables you to start breaking down a lifetime of beliefs around the dangers of the fear of success.

The Good News

The good news for the Half Hearters is that they are great at learning new ideas even if they don't employ them. They are happy where they are (usually because they are un-keen to look too far ahead for fear that they will fail at it!)

Working Towards Success

A client came to me and said they felt their fear of success and that it meant they rarely applied themselves.

From the "And that means" exercise, we were able to see what was the underlining issue. They really feared what other people thought of them. They'd been bullied as a child and in their first job and it had stuck around in their head telling them to just hide in the office and don't stand out. It meant they now felt overlooked and unappreciated.

Dealing with their fear of success and what people thought of them meant they learned to employ communication skills they already knew but were too fearful to use. And then, they got not one but 2 pay rises and promotions!

6. THE INVENTORS

Inventors are awesome to coach because they get results fast. It's a great example of how you can change the results you get in an instant because it's about what you think before what you do.

Inventors create a perception of reality that supports where they are. It means that they don't notice the fear of success that exists at all!

Inventors are likely to say:

- I've tried everything.
- I've no idea how to do this.

Inventors need someone to hold their hand to overcome their fear. Their ability to create, nurture and believe their own version of reality keeps them safe and it makes it very hard to escape on their own.

Strategies to Employ

More than any other archetype, the Inventor has to strip back what they think and find its source. Going it alone is not a great option because the Inventor can constantly recreate reality to support where they are.

Having someone to help them confront what they believe to be true really can help. Don't ask your partner or friend because they just want you to be happy (more than successful) and don't want to see you upset.

I have had hundreds and hundreds of people cry in a coaching session and be mortified by it, but it's in that moment of tears that they have realized what the fear has done to them, how it has stopped them and a complete release that there really is a new way they could think to get what they want.

Don't go it alone, find someone who you can trust to challenge you in a supporting way that suits you. Some people like a kick butt approach and others need a gentle gentle approach – start by thinking what your approach might be.

It's funny how quick the right people and opportunities crop up when you are looking in the right direction.

And most importantly, don't berate yourself for who you are. When you start to break down your perception of reality, most of my clients discover how awesome they really are and their new perception of reality is far better (and quite often instant!)

The Good News

The Inventors don't tend to like looking too closely at their emotions and feelings. If they do, then their perception of reality can get dislodged. So they tend to be strong people.

That strength is so important, it enables you to be resilient and determined. Both of these are critical when you face up to your fears.

Working Towards Success!

I was working with a team of people who had 2 inventors in their group. They weren't very good at coming up with new ideas (like the rest of the team) and didn't like being challenged.

By helping them to see that other perceptions of reality existed for other members of the team, they could start to see that they could choose to see things differently if they wanted to.

The trick was in getting them to appreciate the need for change and then giving them the safe zone to challenge what they thought.

With the right support, they were actually the fastest to adopt new ideas because they could quickly create a reality to support the new way of thinking, cool right?

FINAL THOUGHTS

Of all the fears that attack your life, ultimately their role is to lower your confidence levels, keep you trapped and stop you from what you want in life.

By being brave enough to notice them, you are well on the road to fixing them. Therefore wherever you are today, that's a great starting point, remember that.

HOW TO MOVE FORWARD WHEN YOU'RE STUCK IN A RUT

Through coaching I've helped thousands of people get out of ruts, however, rarely do they say "Hey Mand, I'm stuck in a rut, can you get me out?" It makes it sound like it's so small that you could just rock a bit and out you'd pop like the proverbial cork out of the champagne.

If only it was that easy, right?

If you want to know what a rut really is like, check out the films that stick in your mind. At some stage, the stars are stuck in a rut: Ferris Beuller, Luke Skywalker and Jennifer in Dirty Dancing. And since I love Disney, poor old Rapunzel is seriously trapped, and we aren't talking about the tower and the evil step mum.

Looking through my love of films, these films hook us because we look at how that character goes on a metaphorical of physical adventure, and we think by the time we get out of the cinema:

"It's my time!"

"Let's do this"

"I can achieve anything!"

Only to be at home tucked up doing what you usually do, slowly losing that sense of can do that was so alive in you as you left the movies.

So how do you hang on to the motivation to change and how do you make it happen ensuring you never languish there ever again?

1. TALK ABOUT WHAT YOU'RE GOING THROUGH

Whether it's films, news stories or products, so it is stands to reason the same is true of change in our own lives. You can tap into the power of coaching here to get out of your own rut. The first thing I do with a new client is let them talk and talk and talk. No interruptions.

Words spilling out like they can't wait to escape.

The client often talks pretty much nonstop for 20 minutes, maybe a question here or there to help them keep going and dig deeper but, they talk until their shoulders sag and they often look shattered, worn out. It's almost like a fog lifts and they look at me and usually say something like "Wow, where did all that come from?" or "Sorry, I've done your head in with my life haven't I?"

(And I'd like just a penny for every time I hear "You must think I'm a complete weirdo!" For the record no client is.)

While they may have an idea that something is wrong or life is not flying along as they'd love it to, rarely do they actually verbalise everything that they feel is going on.

Giving yourself permission to talk is very important. We are taught in 21st century life to not moan, to look for the positive, to be happy. Sometimes, it's important to really process the other side of this. In doing this, you can really understand what is happening.

People often give me the biggest window into their mind when they least want to. In coaching, it's often the flippant throw away statement that hides the real issues. The perfect example is a recent client who couldn't see away out of their rut. And for some explanation, I asked "For what reason are you always on someone else's path? Is it better over there? Is it safer? What's going on?" The client looked at me in horror and said "How did you know?"

Coaching has become a very spiritual practice for me and sometimes, I ask questions that feel like they are coming through me rather than out of me. Weird I know, but true. It's these weird questions that usually really help clients. I'm probably just picking up on key words they've used repeatedly and then phrasing it in a way that resonates powerfully with the client.

Another great example was the client that told me about all the possibilities the future held for them, and how it made them feel trapped in a rut and they were fearful to escape. I asked "You know how in fog some people will choose not to go out; and others will take precautions to go out there but go slowly; and others carry on regardless and risk everything, which are you?"

They hadn't once talked about fog, but it was a powerful visual that helped them to decide what they wanted. They realized they wanted to go forward, with caution and that created our plan.

For the client who was always on other people's paths, they realized with tears in their eyes that they'd been petrified for years of getting it wrong. They constantly tried to copy everyone else, and we all know that is not the path to success, joy and happiness don't we?

We created a plan of action and I drew a picture of a sign hammered into the grass saying, "Stick to your path!" It's a visual reminder that helps ensure the client stays on track. Look to create visual reminders in your action plan too.

2. BUILD YOURSELF THE RIGHT NETWORK

Network is your net worth. This has been a powerful phrase for me this year and resonates with so many. If you find that you get stuck in a rut or struggle to escape one, have a look around you. The people you work with, socialize with, even listen to on the radio or share your life with on your phone are all part of your network. And we worryingly seem to forget the value of this.

The network around you can either inspire and nurture you or drag you down and keep you stuck.

Have a look at your social media feed, is it full of great ideas, happy faces, great news, beauty and joy? Or is it full of disturbing things happening on the other side of the world that you couldn't possibly ever have an impact on, and moaning people complaining about governments and celebrities?

I'm not suggesting that you don't take an interest and action on helping to shape the world we live in, however, I am saying you need to ask yourself what your social media feed does for you. How does it make you feel?

I asked this question recently on Facebook and was inundated with negative comments and sadness from people who found social media depressing and soul destroying. Interestingly, the ones that felt like me and loved social media felt connected to people around the world. I have social media friends on the other side of the world who I've never met but feel deeply connected to. We can share in joy; we can comfort when our world sees atrocities and we feel connected.

If your network doesn't feel good for you, then change it. No one needs to know.

We can choose to control who is in our life physically and metaphorically, and that can drastically impact on our ability to get out of the ruts that come up in life.

Ever heard someone say:

"What do you want to do that for?"

"That doesn't sound like much fun, are you sure you want that?"

"You just don't get it do you."

"That can't be done."

These comments (and people) can damage your network's net worth. The right people in your network do the very opposite, they are like the critical eureka moment in our favourite films where our stars realise what they can achieve.

There are so many people around the world I have never met and yet, we've helped each other on those dark "I can't do this days."

I've never been to Tucson, AZ. However, I know I've at least one friend there in Alicia from Energetic Life Healing. While we've never met, we both know we can get in touch if we want advice, support or a proverbial kick up the butt to get where we want to go in life. And I've long distant friends like that around the world. The right network makes such a difference to your ability to steer clear of the ruts of life.

3. DON'T BE TOO PEOPLY*

*(Yes, I know it's a made up word!)

People that try to enslave you to their thinking aren't good for you. A great network respects you whatever you choose to think. Here in the UK, we have faced years of political unrest and divide, and now with Covid – 19 it can seem beyond impossible to escape any rut, it has caused a big rut in many people's lives as they say things like;

"We will move house when Brexit is over."

"I will set up my own business when Brexit is done."

"It's not practical to do that until Brexit is finished.

"It's pointless trying to set up a business now."

"*They* say that it will all be over by Christmas."

"We can't make a decision yet because we don't know what is going to happen."

Too peoply is a saying a friend (funnily enough who started off as a social media friend is now a real friend) said to me once. If I am around people too much, it gets too peoply and I need a break." When I asked about getting stuck in a rut online Abbie Thoms from Polyspiral Website Design said:

"I think we get caught up in our situations and forget to take a step back for some perspective."

Spot on Abbie!

As my friend and Abbie have beautifully sussed, sometimes, the quickest way out of rut is to step back. When I feel stuck on a task or way forward, I know what I must do. A walk on the beach with my dog is important, so much so that I invested in a very expensive coat so that no matter what the weather or temperature I could still go for that walk. The sea air, the solitude and the sound of the waves always help me.

Always, without fail.

Ask yourself when life feels too peoply and you need a new perspective to move forward, what would be on your must do now list? A walk on the beach? Pottering in the garden? Baking a cake? Painting your nails? Daydreaming on YouTube? Reading a book? A DIY project? Even playing a pointless time-wasting game on your phone can be good.

With all of these actions, your brain is given a bit of space to process what you've been working on. So when you feel stuck what will your go to action be?

And please note, working on it some more, is not going to work!

4. PLAN IN A WAY THAT WORKS FOR YOU

If you want to steer clear of a rut, you need to always plan. I like fluid plans, if I have a goal that I can visualize, I'm happy.

I don't need to plan every action. I've learned (the hard way!) that if I plan every finite action, it doesn't work for me; while some clients like everything listed down to details of what they are doing on what day of the week. I have clients that like Excel spreadsheets. Clients that like colourful mind maps. And clients that like mood boards or lists.

We are all so beautifully unique, so before you decide on your plan of action, decide how you will bring your plan alive!

This works so powerfully that for clients that love colour. Without fail, brown is a disliked colour, so I will ask the question in brown "What could stop you?" Because it's a disliked question and a disliked colour, they will work powerfully to steer clear of that result. Which links back to emotions which we talked about at the start. What emotions do you want to evoke when you look at your plan?

5. DON'T PLAN ALONE

Another reason a rut is so tough is because we try and fix it on our own. We think it's the right thing to do, however the 21st Century is teaching us that personally and professionally, we achieve more, are happier, and less stressed if we open up. Planning with the right person or people ensures you:

- Challenge yourself.
- Don't shy away from the things that frighten you.
- Ensure you think creatively.
- Ensure you add ideas that seem ridiculous or crazy.

And this helps you see the big picture in a new way. Which leads us onto...

6. BE AWARE OF YOUR PERCEPTIONS

There is a very good reason why a 2 hour conversation with me can completely change the way someone feels about their life, and who they are and it is down to perceptions.

Perceptions are what shape the world we live in. However, it has always fascinated me that two people can see the same film, visit the say party or explore the same place and feel completely different about it. Our perception of the world we live in and who we are is impacted on by our beliefs, values and experiences. Helping people to adjust their beliefs and respect their values and experiences is a fast way to getting a perspective that helps you instead of keeping you trapped.

7. REALIZE THAT YOU'RE JUST TRAPPED IN LIMBO

If you help someone to explore their rut, it often can drag them down further. They feel trapped by circumstances and say things like:

- "It can't be helped."

- "It's just the way it is".

- "It's just our current circumstances, when this is over we can…"

Watch out for victim talk when it comes to ruts in your own life. Speaking from experience, it is not always easy, yet we can escape the most awful of situations however badly we feel trapped by what we choose to think. Lupus has isolated me from society and destroyed my social life. At times, I would cry because it felt like I was the only person in the world.

Just me and my dog.

If you've ever faced adversity or tough times out of your control, it can feel like a rut because you can't find a way forward. The fastest way forward is not always putting one foot in front of another, it is by monitoring the quality of your thoughts.

I loved the book The Forgotten Highlander by Alistair Urquhart. The true story of a Scottish soldier who faced some of the worse most horrific moments of the second world war. I saw an interview with him years ago where the interviewer asked Alistair "How did you keep going?" and Alistair talked about how they could do what they wanted to his body but they were never getting their hands on his mind!

This was the belief that changed my circumstances. Not medicine, or exercise or diet or friends, but just one thought. Which leads me to the next thing that ensures I never fall into a rut again...

8. PRACTICE GRATITUDE

If you want to get out of a rut, another way to slay the victim mentality is to look for everything you love about your world. Everything you are honoured to have. Everything that makes you feel happy and loved. It is hard to feel trapped when you find yourself experiencing so many positive emotions.

Remember positivity is a great place to start when you want to change something in your life. Blind positivity is not much use, but positivity based on facts is.

I'm more than happy to hear from readers anytime, so do feel free to get in touch via my social media which you can access via www.mandieholgate.co.uk . Let's keep the conversation and the lifehacks going!

SELF AWARENESS IS UNDERRATED: WHY THE CONSCIOUS MIND LEADS TO HAPPINESS

Whether your life is motoring along beautifully or you feel like you're hitting one pot hole after another with constant grief and hardship, there are things you can do to have a better life. One of the things I think we're seeing more and more is moving away from a desire for material riches, and a desire for freedom (emotional and physical.) And instead of seeking things, we are seeking feelings. We want to get away from pain and hurt, guilt and sadness, and want to experience more fulfilment, love and happiness.

Even I read that paragraph and thought "Mandie when did you become a flowers in the hair kind of girl?" However, the fact is we do seem to be craving different things to what I've seen people come to me for coaching for in the past. And one of the most important things we are learning from this shift is that, no matter how fun or fear packed your life, no matter how much you hate and loathe or enjoy and love your life right now, there are things you can do to make it better.

Right now, at this very moment.

Not with more money, a bigger house, a newer car, or a smaller or larger body, not with your boss's job or a house on a beach; today, at this very minute you could create a better life.

Really?

I speak from experience here. In the first half of 2017, I attended three funerals of people far too young. Three members of my family had serious health scares. My hard drive blew up, so did our boiler. (On the coldest week of the year!) It felt like the electric goods around the house were conspiring against us, both of our cars were hit while we weren't even in them within in two weeks. And my beautiful Springer Spaniel fell ill suddenly, and I had to have him put down when my Husband was on the other side of the world.

And that is just some of the stuff that happened in the first half of that year. It was hard to not feel victimized, and like there was some evil deity reigning down a torrent of hell on the Holgate family. And having suffered from severe depression that nearly killed me 16 years ago, I will be honest and say I feared for my mental health.

Despite the feeling of "is this really all happening to us?" that aimed to raise it's ugly head, I managed to stay happy. It become the Holgate mantra that the harder times got, the happier we felt.

How is that possible and why does it matter?

You see no matter what happens on the outside, we can choose what we think and feel on the inside and when we appreciate the power of this self awareness we can dramatically change not just our day, but our futures too.

Now it gets interesting, right?

Have you ever heard the saying "Who got out of bed on the wrong side?" That person moves through their day feeling miserable, frustrated and struggles to hold compelling conversations or get the results they want to. Did it start with these bad results?

No of course not, it started with the thought that created the actions that delivered the results.

Being able to be self aware is a powerful way to power up your happiness, actions and success. It enables you to be in touch with who you truly are.

My own experience taught me that I have a very blessed life (despite the three auto immune diseases and losing my dear old dog.) It reinforced for me that I'm on the right path, going for the right goals for the right reasons. Many people find that despite achieving success in the traditional ways, they still lack happiness and it is highly likely it could come down to not being self aware of what matters to you.

5 POWERFUL STEPS TO BUILD SELF AWARENESS

Here I share my 5 top tips to self awareness and how this power could help you achieve more personally, professionally and emotionally.

1. DROP THE VICTIM ACT

This has been so powerful for so many that I've worked with (including myself). Have you noticed how around some people, you are confident and capable; and around others you feel like a child?

Or maybe you lose your power?

Be aware of how you feel around different people. It is not your job to change people, it is your responsibility to change the way you perceive people and handle them. This is an internal exercise. Maybe you were bullied at school and you still question if people are your friends, and this impacts on your choice of activities and level of trust.

Maybe you had an over critical parent or teacher and still find yourself berating things that you do. Become aware of these beliefs that you may have stored for decades. You don't have to challenge them if that feels too big a step. Just notice them at this stage.

2. RESPECT, ACCEPT AND APPRECIATE WHO YOU ARE

I remember up until only about seven years ago that someone I love dearly would say "You are so over sensitive Mandie!" and for years I saw that as a negative. I actually learned that I was not respecting who Mandie was. How can you achieve the things in life that make you happy, including just pure love for you that leads to internal genuine happiness if you don't respect who you are?

It may sound like a girlie fluffy subject, however by not respecting yourself and understanding your own emotional intelligence, you can seriously damage your chances of achieving. I learned for instance that what I'd seen as oversensitivity was in fact one of the reasons that I find coaching so easy and powerful—I can truly connect on a level that most people miss.

3. LEARN WHAT YOU TRULY VALUE

If you learn to respect, accept and appreciate who you are, you can still find that you have emotional negative attachment to elements of who you are. By learning to hear and listen to your values, you can become more self aware and go for things that really matter to you.

In my book Fight the fear – how to beat your negative mindset and win in life, I recommend the values exercise. It enables you to explore on a subconscious level to learn what really matters to you. This is great for when you fear that you are concentrating on the wrong things in life—often being impacted on by the outside world, rather than hearing and knowing your own values.

4. REFRAME YOUR NEGATIVE THOUGHTS

So after you've learned to accept who you are, you can still find that negativity is impacting on your ability to become self aware. If you have feelings of low value and self worth, it's hard to want to listen to more of your thoughts. Re-framing your thoughts can help.

Listen carefully to your negative thoughts, beliefs and feelings. Don't try and change them, just acknowledge them.

What comes next? Is it a physical thing, an emotion or a belief? By following the flow of this, you can create a negative spiral of what happens to you when you are not self aware. The awesome thing is I've used this process with so many clients to shift them fast into a positive spiral.

On the next 2 pages is an example of how many of us struggle to accept compliments.

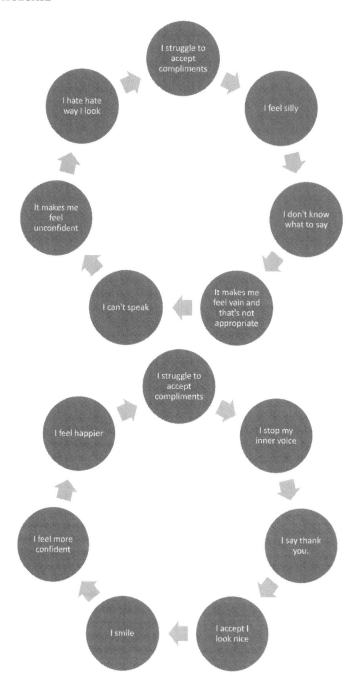

5. DITCH THE SHALLOW SELF DEVELOPMENT

With a growing appreciation around the world that our minds impact on our success, alas there are some that are exploring this subject on a very superficial level. While any level is better than nothing, you need to do your homework if you really want to be self aware. Expecting results by osmosis or by reading motivational posters is not enough.

Aristotle, Einstein and so many others have indeed said powerful things about our minds and our ability to achieve true happiness, creativity and success. However remember that at their core they were people of action too.

By always assessing your self awareness, you can learn to not just respect who you are but to trust this true version of you. And that could be incredibly powerful on so many levels.

HOW TO EFFECTIVELY SET GOALS IN LIFE TO GET WHERE YOU REALLY WANT TO BE

I'd love 1 penny for every time I've been able to help someone achieve their goals in life fast with the idea I'm going to share in this chapter. It's that frequent that I'd be a millionaire a good few times over!

Often people looking to get somewhere in life advise that they have read 100's of books, watched tons of Ted talks, attended workshops and masterclasses around the world, invested in programmes, wrote a journal, changed their lifestyle, and even transformed what time they get up in the morning; and yet miraculously they've not achieved their goals.

What can possibly have stopped them when they've put so much effort into achieving more? And can you really share one thought and change a person's life?

In a coaching conversation, I've watched a client have a look that is a mishmash of horror, elation, eureka and annoyance as they realize that it is this one thing that will define their chances of success. And that it has been stood in their way like a giant rock for years.

Here I share what that is and how to ensure you get the rocks out of the way of your ability to set life goals that get you where you want to go.

1. LOOK FOR THE THINGS THAT RESONATE WITH YOU

It can seem obvious that if you are looking to achieve big and get somewhere in life, then you will take the time and money to invest in finding the best ways of achieving that. The issue with this is that your brain didn't get the memo on what was supposed to work.

Let me give you an example (I could give you thousands!):

A client says that they have been getting up at 5am because they read that this was the Golden Hour if you want to achieve big and they shared with me what you were supposed to do in your Golden Hour.

I asked "Is this working?"

They replied "well I am reading more and I'm learning, but I'm grumpy as a bear by the afternoon and rowing with the kids and don't even get a cuddle with my partner in the morning"

I questioned "So, is it working?"

They answered "I suppose in some aspects yes but in most aspects no."

"So why are you still doing it?"

They retorted "Because the book said it was good to do!"

I then asked them a personal question, unrelated to business, careers or success "Do you like the mornings?"

They laughed "Oh gosh no, I'm a night owl, I hate the mornings!"

So why were they going out of their way to utilize a system that relied on them going against the very fibre of their being?

When I raised this to them, they looked like someone had just thrown a bucket of ice cold water over them. It would obviously never work long term because they were fighting who they were.

Remember while these books are selling in their millions and these speakers are amazing, what works for one does not by definition mean it will work for you. You have to work with ideas, tools and techniques that play to the person you are.

It is no good fighting who you are, eventually your brain will fight back. It never got the memo, it didn't know this was the new way of working and it is not going to play ball.

There is an argument that you need to stick with things to make your habits change. While I agree with this in principle, if the ideas encourage you to stray massively away from the human you are, it is highly likely you will fail.)

So how do you fix it?

Look for the things that resonate with you. If you hate things structured and like to be free flowing then look for ideas that empower you to think and work in that way.

Another great example is the client who had a big figure in their head that they wanted to earn. And they were going to do it.

The only issue was that the journey was practically killing them. They were working stupid hours with little down time and their health, personal and social life were suffering, no big deal right?

Short term losses for long term gains?

Except this person performed the Values Exercise from my book Fight the fear – that looks at the 12 biggest fears that impact on success, and discovered that the top 3 values that mattered most to them were actually caring about others, friends and exercise.

Making money was right down the list at number 8! While it's fine to go for a goal that is not your top value, you do need to still honour the values and the things that make you, you.

When you don't, you can hit all sorts of barriers and road blocks to getting what you want, so don't fight who you are, your brain just didn't get the memo.

2. FILTER OUT WHAT YOU DON'T WANT AND BE CAREFUL OF WHAT YOU ALLOW IN

Big goals, bucket lists and ambitions — the problem is that while you are busy creating these plans so you achieve them, your brain processes everything you experience.

Everything from the dog asleep by your feet, the trees moving just at the edge of your vision. The couple arguing in the corner, the coffee stain on the edge of your cup, the siren in the distance, the beep from your phone – everything!

Whatever is around you, your brain is processing it on some level. While in itself that's amazing, it also means that you need to be clear on what you say to your brain. Not only is it processing every smell and sound it is processing every thought, belief and word you hear. That's a lot!

Filter out the stuff you don't want and be careful what you allow in. My Mum used to say "Treat advice like water into a sponge, let everything in just wring out what you don't want." This is very apt for this top tip.

When looking to achieve your goals, people will share ideas, advice and books you "Must read!" Let it all come to you and then genuinely ask:

"Does this fit the human I am?"

"Does this play to my strengths?"

"Is this the best use of my time to get me where I want to go?"

While many people love videos and inspirational events, if you prefer to be on your own with a good book or speaking one to one with someone, which is more likely to help you understand the power of your brain, create powerful actions and work towards your long term goals in life?

Learn to wring out the stuff that is not relevant to you.

3. KEEP YOUR GOAL AS SIMPLE AS IT CAN BE

Your brain can process 400 billion bits of information a second and yet we only seem to be aware of around 2000[1] So if this is true, you need to be aware that what you want is not the only thing your brain is working on.

If you want your goals to feature in the top actions to process, you need to keep it simple.

For your desires to feature above anything else, you need to make it something easy to remember and keep at the front of your brain.

Reword where you want to be and what you want to achieve into 1 sentence. Make it a powerful sentence that enables you to "see" your goal.

To achieve this you will need to break the goal down. (Which is important for the next top tip too.) Write down the answers to these thoughts:

Think of everything that matters to you about this goal.

Consider all the emotions you want to feel and don't want to feel.

Where will you be when you've achieved this goal. Will your home look different? Will your workplace look the same? Will you be driving a different car?

Will you look different? What colour will your hair be (is it going to take you 30 years to achieve and you've gone grey or will you have found a new level of confidence and dyed your hair pink like you always wanted to?)

What will tell you that you've achieved that goal?

How will it impact on your life? Your bank balance? Your relationships? Your career? Your happiness? Your hobbies?

When you've considered everything that could feature in your 1 sentence that summarizes your goal, then look to create a sentence that does that. Make it a sentence with:

An end result. This helps your brain remember where you want to get to and gives it a specific place to end up.

Precise actions. This helps your brain to see what process you want to carry out and enables you to see if you are getting there, so you can analyse your actions results and where you are in the process.

Something to strive for not strain for. Your goal should aim to make you strive further than you would naturally choose to. Imagine reaching your arm out to reach something that feels a little tight in your arm as you find yourself thinking "Can I reach this?" However a word of caution here – A goal that over strains you can drain you picture.

Great sentence choices could be:

"By the 25th of September this year I will have achieved my goal to own a property in X town with 2 bedrooms at a cost of XXX"

"By the end of March next year I will have earned an average of xxxxxx a month by increasing sales of my products by 33% incorporating more interactive marketing techniques that engage with a wider audience of 10,000 additional people online."

Notice these goal sentences have:

Precise outcomes

Dates to work towards (ever noticed how some people have months to achieve something and still scrap around getting it done the night before the deadline?)

Measurable quantities

Precise actions to take.

Ironic, isn't it that the brain likes it simple? And to make it simple, I have to explain this tip in more detail than any other top tip!

However, what I'm doing is sharing with you a little of the science of why coaching works and how to get these tools in your every day life to power up your chances of getting where you want in life. So do take the time to go through this process.

4. REPEATEDLY TAKE ONLY A FEW ACTIONS

Once you have your goal sentence, go back to all of the words you wrote down for Number 1 and write down everything you could do to achieve that goal.

At this stage, this is not what you will do, this is what you could do. By doing this, you are stretching (not straining) your brain to think further than it would normally about your actions.

The problem we have is our brain is processing so much that a lot of what it does is automatic (habit). To create new powerful actions, we need to break past that automatic way of thinking.

As I explain it to clients:

You are going to start by telling me the obvious ideas and the ideas that you mull over at 2 am but don't do. You are also likely to share the ideas that you've spent months agonising over whether you should do them or not but something always seems to stop you.

And after that, we can fight through the assumptions of what can be achieved. Overrule the doubts and limiting beliefs about your abilities and get on to finding the real actions that will get you to where you want to go.

Then when you have a long list of things you could do, choose a maximum of 5 actions that you will do to achieve your goal. It doesn't mean you won't do more of the ideas on this list, just that at this stage you are creating priority to concentrate on a maximum of 5 goals.

5. BREAK THE ACTIONS DOWN INTO SMALLER ONES

When you've completed the above top tip, you need to work out how you're going to accomplish those 5 actions only ever have a maximum of 5 actions at any one time.

For me, I put them on a small 8 cm squared post it note, because in this way I know I'm not overloading my to do list.

The brain really hates it when you give it too much to process. It's like trying to load a basket in the supermarket with a trolleys worth of shopping; stuff falls out!

Break down those 5 actions. This is useful for a number of reasons:

Firstly, it helps your brain stay focused on the action you are taking and the reasons why.

Secondly, it enables you to tick things off of your to do list. This always has a sense of achievement and makes us feel good.

In fact clever scientists tell us that dopamine is released when we achieve something (however small) and our brains love a hit of dopamine. It is a neurotransmitter that our brain produces and enables us to stay focused, motived and get things done.

So by breaking your goals down, you are rewarding your brain with a hit of the good stuff and that gives you the much needed boost to keep going. Especially if you are incorporating new things into your life that are challenging you to think and act in a new way.

Lastly, when it comes to breaking it down you don't need to write a list. If you're a lover of mind maps, then create a simple version of this. If you love a spreadsheet – go for it. And if you like it visual, draw it.

Whatever you do, make sure the 5 actions from the above top tip are broken down and visually near you so that you are able to keep focused on what you want.

6. HAVE A LIST OF WHAT TO DO NOW

Your brain may not appreciate the need to get on with the "Now" Goals but your success does.

I've often seen clients struggling to achieve what they want to because they've not factored in that little thing called life. For instance, you may have a big ambition but you've not factored in spending time with family and friends.

Big deal, right? Short term sacrifice for long term gains, right?

While in principle I agree, the fact is that while you power on to your big ambitions, your brain is still busy processing that sulky look on your child's/friends/partners/mum's face that says "You never have time any more." And while you can justify that it's "for the best" in your head, you can create this automatic subconscious process of thoughts that is negative.

I've seen clients realize that the reason they've not getting to where they want to go is because their brain has started to scupper their own success! It has rationalized that if they keep working this hard, the people they love will never love them again.

They realize in their head there are thoughts like "My child/friend/partner/mum thinks I don't care any more and they will leave me. I can't afford to achieve this I could lose everyone!"

I've seen the same happen when redecorating the office/kitchen/kids room gets demoted for something else. Or when someone drops their weekly trip to the gym or yoga session. Both of these examples create negative emotions that subconsciously start to eat away at us.

So if you want to achieve big, have a list of Now goals too. In my experience I help my clients prioritize the top Now goal and the top action for the big ambition. And they don't move onto the next action on either list until both of the first actions are achieved.

7. GET A COACH TO HELP YOU

I hate to say it but going it alone is going to make it harder. You need to find someone that's going to help you get where you want to go. And that is why a coach is so powerful.

A coach is someone that will:

Listen so you can brain dump.

Empty your head of all your thoughts, what you've done so far, your worries, your failures, your concerns, everything and they list it and are ready to recap with you so you remember what is really going on.

Create the space to find a new better way of working and living.

So you can process everything that has been happening, what doesn't seem to be working, and find a way forward.

They are going to challenge you

The problem with turning to friends, family and colleagues is that they all have their own views, ideas, beliefs, values and experiences. And no two people are alike, as such while they may care deeply about you getting what you want, they may try and steer you away from tough choices. Your coach won't. If anything, they will encourage you to find the things you fear or steer clear of and help you find a way to remove those obstacles so they never feature in your life again!

A coach is going to cheer lead you

Sometimes what we need more than anything is a reminder of

how awesome we are. The problem is that if you go around asking your friends for that and you can look needy, arrogant or a bit egocentric. However, we all need a cheer leader.

This is not just to inflate your ego, but it's remind you of how you achieve. We all have natural ways of behaving that works for us and by having a cheer leader on your side you can stay motivated and concentrate on remembering what helped you achieve in the past and how to migrate those skills, beliefs and actions to this moment in your life.

A coach will keep you on track

Alas we are so easily distracted. And even those going for big goals in life can find that they are on a completely different path and have no idea how it happened!

Quite often, someone has suggested a great idea to you and while it is a great idea, you need to challenge yourself "Does this great idea fit into my big goal or is this a distraction from it?" With a coach, they ask a lot of questions so you can really understand your way of thinking and its impact on you and your results.

If you find yourself easily distracted, other good questions to ask are "For what reason do I get distracted?" and "What is it that I don't want to face in my own path to success?" Facing your fears and hidden negative assumptions is a massive part of getting to where you want to go and a real power of a coach.

A coach helps you retrain your brain

When I first got my dog, she would bark at everything and when I say everything I mean everything. A leaf in the garden would get as much yapping noise as the postman. And for someone who has always had big dogs, even though my dog is more like something Jim Henson created for Muppets, she is not going to destroy my seaside peace and quiet (or my neighbours)

What has this to do with why you need the right coach to help you achieve your personal goals? Well, my dog was on her own agenda and she hadn't had anyone explain to her that this wasn't the best way of behaving. (The last owners had got rid of her because she barked too much) She needed to retrain so that she could be happy, but no one had told her this.

A coach will confront you with the hard lessons in life. In a nice way, I like to say "I kick butt, with love!" My dog is welcome to bark when the doorbell chimes or if she thinks there is an intruder but not at the bird having a drink of water or the leaf that flutters across the lawn.

Be cautious of whose agenda you are on, does it serve the other party more than you? Will it help you get the result you want?

And a word of caution about your coach:

If they do more talking than listening, they are not coaching you. Your coach is there to help you process everything in your head, and that can't happen if someone is adding more to your brain.

A coach listens for over 60% of the conversation. It is an unusual conversation because the coach's view is irrelevant, the only person that matters in the conversation is you.

So if you aren't getting that from the person you rely on to help you achieve your big goals, then they aren't coaching you to success, they are trying to tell you how to be successful.

And while mentoring and consulting have their place in helping people to get where they want to go in life, to really get there you need to find your own answers. And hopefully in this chapter I've helped you do just that.

[1] ^ Scientific American: Gut Feelings www.scientifi-camerican.com/article/gut-feelings-the-second-brain-in-our-gastrointestinal-systems-excerpt

[2] ^ Exploring Your Mind: The Heart Has Neurons Too www.exploringyourmind.com/the-heart-has-neurons-too/

[3] ^ Mike Bundrant: The A-H-A Solution

HOW TO OVERCOME YOUR BIGGEST ENEMY IN LIFE: FEAR

Have you ever heard someone say "Me? I'm rubbish at mathematics!"

or "It's no good asking me I've always struggled with grammar"?

These are two perfect examples of the chosen thoughts we allow to hang out in our minds that dismember our goals and our results.

So many of us enable the wrong thoughts in our minds and our brain is only too happy to deliver exactly what we ask for. The damage is caused when we don't realise we've been asking for the wrong things.

You see, our brain is a clever old bunch of cells. It's highly likely you've heard of the exercise where you are asked to not think of a pink elephant… and weirdly there in your head is a pink elephant! Or of Pavlov's dogs, who could be encouraged to salivate just on hearing a bell ring. Even now I could say to you "Don't imagine a lemon being cut in half and the juice being squeezed down your throat", and you'd start to realise "Hey I'm producing more saliva". How is that possible?

Because our brains WILL deliver what we ask for.

When it comes to performance we have to choose our words carefully. If you appreciate the above and accept that we are easily suggestible creatures, then by nature it stands to reason that I can give you some top tips and tools to help you perform better just based on what words you are choosing to think.

You see, if words can impact what your body does it can also impact the results you achieve, and the standard to which you perform at.

HOW FEAR SCREWS
YOU UP

How is it that one person can relish the opportunity to stand on a stage in front of 5000 people, and another would rather have their spleen burst before it was their turn? (And trust me as someone who used to have a very physical fear of public speaking and who now adores it and coaches people out of that fear, I really know what that fear is like.) If we allow such a fear to fester and hang out in our minds then guess what that can do to your performance?

Let's stick with the public speaking fear since it is still one of the top fears in the world. We are still more scared of speaking than dying. Crazy right?

You are asked to speak to a large audience and the opportunity has the potential to rocket your career. If you fear public speaking then the overriding thoughts are around the fear... instead of the ideal results you want to get.

For instance, instead of thinking:

"This is the opportunity I've been waiting for and it's going to rocket my success"

You are more likely to be thinking:

"Oh no the biggest opportunity of my life and I'm going to screw it up."

Now remember our brain likes to keep us happy. So, if you are thinking the first positive thought guess what you are likely to get? And what about the second one?

"That's all very well and good Mandie but it's a fear. It's real, it's tangible. It shuts my throat, makes me shake, sweat and I struggle to remember my name let alone an entire speech!" you say.

And from many years' experience of helping people overcome those fears I know that this is exactly what fear relies on. It relies on you accepting the feelings, and accepting the physicality of it. It relies on you accepting those negative emotions and really experiencing them on a level that causes you to never question them. And that is the key.

To increase your performance success, you have to question your thoughts. Not all fears are obvious. Some can hide out in your subconscious for years and it's only when you work on them that you become aware of a fear that has been impacting on your success.

Everyone Has Fears, Even Those Who Look So Tough

Don't believe me?

Only recently I had someone who I've admired for a long time on an international level say to me that it was not until they read chapter 3 of my book (Fight the fear) that they realised something had been impacting their success for years. That something was the action of picking up the phone. How can picking up the phone kill your performance?

Let's break it down by thinking about what happens if you choose your actions according to your thoughts. So, if you think picking up the phone is going to interrupt someone's day, make them less likely to say "Yes" and want to hear what you have got to say, are you likely to revert to an email?

On the other hand, what if you accept that you are a valuable person who has every right to speak to someone on the phone because you have something useful to say that could be very relevant and interesting? What are the chances you will pick up the phone?

So how do you revert to positive thinking and override the fears that damage your performance?

4 TIPS TO OVERRIDE YOUR FEARS

Adjust Your Assumptions

What assumptions are you making and are they good or bad for you? For instance, if you assume that mistakes are opportunities to learn, then you will go for it with all your heart. You will trust that even failure has its benefits and use them effectively to power up your performance. On the other hand, if you believe that failure is dangerous and damages your reputation and success then you are likely to shy away from the opportunities that can risk failure. With fear, you have to think like the superhero in a movie. Be prepared to step into situations that you fear with trust that you can do this. You don't see superhero's look at the big evil 20-foot bad guy and think "Mmm I don't think I will protect mankind today, he looks a bit scary."

Remember No One Really Cares

A big reason that fear can impact your performance and thus success is because we imagine what people are thinking. Ironically, it's not usually true. We assume that everyone is thinking about us, and yet they are much more likely to be thinking about themselves — "what's for tea", "what they are going to get their Mom for her birthday" or "why did I wear these shoes, they're far too tight". However, remember that fear relies on negativity holding us in place and so if you just learn to accept that everyone is thinking their own thoughts and are as obsessed with them as you are yours, you can stop allowing incorrect thoughts into your head. And as one business friend said to me once "Mandie, you have no right to the thoughts in other people's heads."

Shift Your Focus

Fear loves us to repeat patterns. So, if you have thoughts in your head that say "this won't work", or "I'm scared of the end results" —then your brain will do all it can to prove you right.

Therefore, if you can have a stronger new direction to focus your attention on the fear will reduce and eventually dissipate. For instance, let's go back to the fear of public speaking (You can replace this fear with one of your own!) If you fear public speaking and focus on what you fear, that is what you will get. On the other hand, if you have a clear goal in sight then that is what you are more likely to get. That means you need to work out what you want. What do you want? What is the goal? Where do you want this to lead? By answering these questions with your true passions and desires your brain has a positive direction to aim for, and not the fear routed patterns of the past.

Don't Be Afraid of Looking Stupid

Closely connected to the fear of what people think is the fear that you will make a fool of yourself. Thus, if you fear what people think and/or making mistakes and getting it wrong then fear again gets to overpower you. Think about a time you've felt stupid for saying or doing something.

What happened next?

Then answer, "How did that make you feel?"

And then from that ask yourself "Did that result in a feeling or an action?"

And then answer, "what happened next?"

In this way, you can start to build up a picture of the automatic path way connected to this fear. How you fall into old patterns that have not served you powerfully, and allowed fear to hold its power of you.

(And yes, this process can be used on any fear, I call this a negative spiral.)

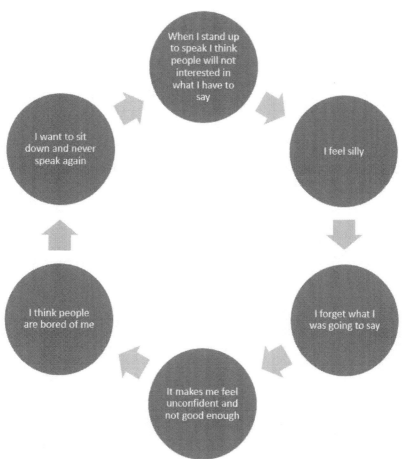

Once you build a picture of what is happening in your old state you can learn to see what thoughts and feelings create what actions.

For instance, if you stood up for yourself and spoke up and that led to you feeling inferior, did that then lead to you not taking on the project that was offered to you, because you feared getting it wrong?

Understanding the thoughts that create the actions means that you then decide to create a new thought, and that will lead to new actions. But again, this really needs a powerful focus and goal to help you achieve.

Ultimately fear is allowed to impact our performance because we've learnt to trust fear. Fear is useful in that it keeps us safe, however there aren't too many woolly mammoths on the streets anymore. So when fear is given too much power it damages our success. Learn to challenge and stop assuming.

And most importantly trust that you can do this, you can give yourself all the proof of your successes to tell you this.

And I will leave you with this thought: Why do we assume what if we are awesome at something then everyone else can do that too? While if we can't do something we are idiots because everyone else can do it?

You see, fear really does wish to damage your success. So, it's time to challenge it.

HOW TO STOP RACING THOUGHTS WHEN YOUR MIND WON'T LET UP

If you could see a diagram of my brain and you could imagine every line was a thought, it would look like you'd given a room full of 4 year olds crayons and told them to draw on the floor of a huge room. I don't think one thing at a time. As my family say "I think Auntie Winn".

My Auntie Winn could think about 30 conversations at the same time and expect you to jump from discussing world politics to the qualities of a good rock cake in less time than it took to the boil the kettle. Apparently, I do that to my husband too, I can often hear him saying "I know you think we've had this conversation today, however I've a feeling you're giving me an answer to a conversation we had last Thursday in the hot tub!"

So, racing thoughts and me are best friends, or are we?

I realized that while I can be thinking a thousand thoughts at once, I don't suffer from overwhelm, how is that? How to stop racing thoughts?

In this chapter, I want to share how to silence your mind, create some space and why it's so good to do personally and professionally.

DOES EVERYONE HAVE RACING THOUGHTS?

Before I share these ideas, I want to share something that really shocked me.

I decided to ask my social media friends if they "suffered" from a racing mind as so many of my clients do. The response was a little alarming:

100% of respondents said they felt overwhelmed with many saying they felt like their mind was crazy and "Switching off? What's that!"

From my over busy friends' minds, it seems that it doesn't just impact on your mind, it also impacts on your actions, what you get done in a day and even your ability to get a decent nights sleep!

It really is time to get that mind to let up and give you some time isn't it!

So how can we fix this?

Here I'm going to share a few tools to help you put the brakes on, calm your mind and achieve more without letting any of the important thoughts slip through your head.

How to Stop Racing Thoughts In Your Mind

1. LISTEN TO YOUR MIND – THINK LIKE A PRO

I realized that one of the skills I've learned since I became ill with Lupus is that, I've learned to think in the most powerful way possible.

Every thought is processed. I've been using this practice for so many years and I appreciate that I don't consciously do this anymore. However, at the start, you will have to structure your thinking. When I say processed, I mean I am aware of the nature of my thoughts.

For instance:

RACING THOUGHTS
LISTEN TO YOUR MIND - THINK LIKE A PRO

THE THOUGHT...	MY RESPONSE TO IT...
"Ooo, i need to reply to Mr X"	"Is Mr X expecting a reply today and does it fit my money making/success/sanity saving/critical tasks for the day?"
"I know that phoning Mrs X is not urgent however I don't want them to think I don't care or I don't consider what they need as important."	I can easily worry about what people are thinking about me and my actions and this thought can be common. By creating the right boundaries from day one with my clients/friends/connections and even family they know what I'm capable of, they know my preferred way of working and responding and I know theirs too. This means we build respect and have boundaries. They also know if they want/need something urgently I have this amazing device called aphone!
"I should be doing this not that..."	How many times do you finanlly run a bath, finish work on time, walk the dog or finanlly make it to the gym or meet up with friends only to feel guilty for doing it? Crazy right? If you've going to do something, do it. I've seen many a coaching client who's admitted to the guilt of doing something they love and as I've discovered guilt is not for anyone, so ditch it.
"I can't believe I've still not achieved that!"	Is this a beneficial response to this? Will it motivate me to take the action I've not been taking?

CHALLENGE THE QUALITY OF YOUR THOUGHTS
THEY COULD DAMAGE YOUR ACTIONS AND RESULTS

I could go on, however do you get the idea?

Listen to what your head has to say and then process it. If you don't take the time to learn to do this, then ask yourself what impact this could have on your brain space, actions and results?

2. CALM THE MIND

When you've learned to actually listen to all that chatter in your head, it's time to calm the mind.

Listening does not automatically equate to it all magically disappearing. And calming the mind doesn't require a tropical paradise, a massage and the sounds of nature to achieve a bit of brain space.

For some clients, they've discovered the fastest way to shut their brains up is to crank up the music, so they literally can't hear anything except their favourite song.

For others, 5 minutes in the garden is enough to make them rethink. I wouldn't say there's only one thing that takes you to a calm place, Create a list of at least 12 physical things you can do to calm your mind down. Create that list now so that when you have too much in your head, you don't have to try and think of something else!

That way, whether you have a hyper mind with excitement, anger, too much going on or feeling completely overwhelmed by life, you have different ideas to work.

3. THE HI, WELCOME, GOOD MORNING GAME

For me, sometimes a walk under the big oak trees is enough; other times, I just find myself getting even more flustered as the thoughts fight for my attention. On those occasions I've found this really simple exercise quietens my mind and makes me smile:

It's so simple and yet works every time for me. All I do is visualize 10 people that I've met that week and visualize the first word I said to them. I've usually said something like "Great to see you" or "Hello" or "Welcome to my event!"

I love meeting people and I host many different kinds of events, so people are pleased to see me and we are looking forward to our time together. What a great set of emotions and feelings to recreate in my head.

How could you use my welcome exercise to remind you of something in your week that makes you feel good? (This also works on ear worms too!)

4. FOCUS THE MIND

When a coaching client arrives, they tend to start our session by talking so fast that I'm not sure even they can hear half of what they're saying! After about 20 minutes, they are out of breath like they've been for a run, and their shoulders seem a little lighter as they've dumped the contents of their head on to me.

What is happening when a client does this is they are:

Becoming more aware of what is going on in their head. Sometimes actually hearing the truth for the first time themselves!

Then by working with me I can put everything in front of them metaphorically so they can work out what to work on and what to dump. I call it ditch it or deal with it. And it works wonders on "To do" lists too!

Noticing how everything in their head impacts on them — physically and emotionally.

Challenging the beliefs they are holding around their perception of reality.

And that's just for starters! Read on for the next step, but before you do imagine you were sat before me and were and were offloading – what would you say? How are you going to store this information on paper so that it gets out of your head?

5. CREATE A PLAN OF ACTION

Once you can see what is going on, you can create a plan of action that moves you forward.

Focus means "the main or central point of something, especially of attention or interest" and this is what you need to calm an overwhelmed head of racing thoughts.

While you may not have a coach to work with, create some ways to empty everything out of your head and focus on what you need/want to do. These could include:

Arrange to meet with a friend or colleague and agree that "without judgement" they will listen and not interrupt. Agree that you will donate an hour to enable them to do the same.

One Facebook friend told me that their "cure to a racing mind" was to "disappear to bed with a pen and notebook to write it all down." While in theory that is a good idea, I asked them if this worked for them, and they said sometimes. Could that be because they've waited until bedtime to process everything and get it out, instead of dealing with it when it was really a problem?

Journaling can store up a lot of negative emotion if we keep reading it, so pay attention to how your notes make you feel. Is it really beneficial to you or do you need to change the way you write?

Make the time to focus. Do you need to put it in the diary or will you naturally make the time to do this?

Create a list of all the things you could do for all the things you have whirling around in your head. Make it a long list. Dismiss nothing.

Play the ditch it or deal with it game. So often what we think we should be stressing about is actually someone else's definition of important, therefore ask yourself "does this really matter to me?

6. LESS ON YOUR TO DO LIST

Years ago, people would answer "How are you?" with "I'm fine, thanks" or "I've had a bad cold but I'm getting better now, thanks!" However today's reply is far more likely to be "Busy, how are you?"

Many of us have a busy mind because we are so busy. More and more I'm being asked to help professionals and organization to create coach-able strategies to manage their time. Here's a few of those ideas to help you with your racing mind:

Stop over thinking things.

We often over think how long a task that we hate doing is going to take and so put it off and thus it gets to stick around in your head!

Set a timer and know how long a task takes. Many clients have been able to clear a whole task from their head because their perception of its impact on their day and productivity has been changed.

Allow more time.

Contrary to the first top tip, we also underestimate how long other things take to do, usually the things we enjoying doing!

If you know a job will take an hour, allow 1.5 hours. This means if it doesn't take that long, you've just made some brain space for yourself too, so it's a win win situation.

Choose your words wisely.

Have you ever noticed how many sayings we have around words

related to time?

"I really want some Me time".

"I never have the time".

"I know you've got a lot on, but make the time".

"I don't want to spend my time telling you what to do", etc, etc.

Ask yourself if your choice of words free up your mind or make it even busier?

Don't get side-tracked.

We all have alarms and reminders that ping up at us. Even our household appliances now bleep at us saying "Hey, I'm ready, give me your attention!"

Turn them off.

If you know you have a lot on, choose what you can hear carefully. Just like the person turning the music up so they can't hear their own thoughts. Our ability to process what is going on in our heads can be impacted on by the email ping or the notification sounds.

I have seen presentations where we've been told the best course of action is Eisenhower's matrix for time management, which asks you to place every task (or thought) into a grid. The blocks are labelled: Urgent, less urgent, important and less important.

While I've seen clients create their own version of this to great success. I've also seen new clients who have told me that it takes them hours to complete the grid and so they get no work done and end up with even more flying around inside their heads!

That's enough to drive anyone insane! What works for one person does not mean it will work for you. You could try relabelling Eisenhower matrix as my clients to make it personal to you, to encourage you to use it.

Personally I use the 10 day week – a plan I created for a client that is very popular with many readers – you can get that for free on my website – www.mandieholgate.co.uk I hope it helps you too.

Alternatively, there is an app for everything. What about finding an app that enables you to empty your head. I love "To Do" for enabling me to create some space in my head. In this way, you can put to one side thoughts while you concentrate on what is important right now. And when your head starts filling up you can quickly jot those thoughts down and get on with what matters.

7. DITCH THAT GUILT

And lastly, if you have a brain that is running away with you, ditch the guilt because I wouldn't mind betting, you'll free up a lot of space with that 1 action!

Guilt is one of those emotions that causes us to process things again and again and again. Look for the guilt in your thoughts, analyse why it exists and get rid of it.

FINAL THOUGHTS

It's totally normal if you find your thoughts racing in your mind all the time. What you need to do is to really listen to your thoughts and take some concrete actions about those thoughts.

Forcing yourself to silence those thoughts is not the most efficient way in the long run. It is time to face these thoughts and find what works best for you to deal with these racing thoughts because that could lead to brain space, a positive mindset and a new way of thinking which leads to more success too. Worth some time right?

HOW TO STOP LIVING IN FEAR AND START STEPPING OUT OF YOUR COMFORT ZONE

I think I may know why we are so obsessed with super heroes – good versus evil.

Good overcoming no matter what — no matter how big, scary or evil the arch enemy.

It's because it symbolizes how we wish it could be in the real world.

Imagine it…your life is now a movie…

You have music in the background because you are off to work/college/meet friends and your life is pretty normal (all appears well) then on screen, we get a few scenes where your life looks great.

You water your plants (or shrug at your ability to kill anything green), walk the dog, feed the fish, kick back with a good book or hugging a loved one on the sofa with a bucket of popcorn, then all hell breaks loose…

Within 20 minutes, if your life were a film you are feeling, like nothing could ever be the same again and that no one understands what you are going through.

Fear is not the word that springs to mind. It's more likely to be:

- Why me?
- Life will never be good again.
- I can't fight this.
- I don't know where to start.
- This is too big.
- I can't do this alone.
- My life is over.
- We are all doomed!

If your life were a movie, then it's all fine (you really don't need to worry) because at this stage in your film life, when life is so all consumingly going in the wrong way with no way out and death is likely imminent, along comes:

A) A scientist who can't necessarily get you back to "Normal" but can make you a nifty suit and help you become a super hero that everyone loves; after some quirky, funny and lesson learning scenes where you get a few things wrong but learn tons.

B) A rich tycoon who already has a team of super heroes they secretly work with, can see true potential in you (after the "you're rough around the edges kid" scene) they introduce you to the other superheroes and you learn that it doesn't matter what you are like; you will find a network of people that will love respect, trust and help you.

C) An evil so big that everything you've ever believed in as at risk of the worst case scenario, therefore no matter how petrified you are, you somehow find a way to save the world (and your pot plant, dog and/or loved one).

Okay back to reality.

Alas there are not many super heroes' around (if you know otherwise – I can keep a secret), however I think we feel more than ever we need to feel that there is a solution.

Life is fun exciting, challenging (in a good way) fast paced, energized and a ton of other awesome things – but it's also overwhelming, scary and sometimes feels like you are fighting a super villain and you don't have the super hero kit to get through it.

I've never had a client ask me to help them make them a super hero, however I've had plenty ask me to help them feel more in control of their life – and I think that is something we all desire to some degree.

Control of our lives can be eradicated when we feel frightened, un-powerful and like we are trapped in our lives. And often the first sign that we actively recognize is a comfort zone or stress.

But if you think back to our super heroes, no matter how trapped they are, they always find a way out. A solution that no one ever thought could work and that's often what coaching is about – coming to a problem and looking at it in a unique way that enables you to find solutions to fight fear and get out of your comfort zones. And you won't need a scientist, a rich tycoon or a devastating intergalactically incident to find those solutions.

I want to share with you some of the winning techniques I've used with my clients to help you too.

1. Rethink the Question "Am I Weird?"

I've had so many clients ask me this question, I think I should call my next book "Am I weird"!

Everyone thinks that the way they are responding, acting, feeling and thinking is unique; that they are the only person to feel like they can't face work or their friends or their day because of a fear or a comfort zone.

We all have times like this and it's important to remember 2 things:

There is no such thing as normal in my book

Everyone is just who they are. It doesn't need analysing or questioning if you like who you are. Or if who you are serves you well, respects those around you. And if giving you the life, career, and happiness you want, then no, it's not weird. And it's all good.

The issue becomes when you find yourself trying to compare

your weirdness (or lack thereof) to everyone else and how that then impacts on you.

Weird is good

Check out the best characters in film, book, or TV, and you are likely to see that someone else has tried to insult them with the term "weird".

Weird is used when you want to suggest that someone or something is different. Different is not bad, the hard bit is finding the confidence to be who you are – to embrace your differences and your weirdness.

A little useful side note – according to the Oxford English Dictionary:[1]

"Weird – The adjective (late Middle English) originally meant 'having the power to control destiny'"

And who wouldn't want that?

Truly, hear me when I say – embrace your weird.

2. LISTEN UP

Just as the newly discovered superhero struggles to accept their super skills, limitations or fears, so do you have to do the same. And if you strip back any successful story (fictional or real), you will discover it's not a magic potion or a superior race that enables the hero to achieve success, it starts with who they listen to.

How many times in your life have you heard yourself saying:

Why didn't I listen to my gut instinct?

Why didn't I listen to my Mum/Aunt/Friend/Boss?

Just as being weird in its original meaning meant to be able to control destiny until you can actually do that, you do need to learn who to listen and when to listen.

Here's how to take action on this:

Listen to yourself (sometimes)

I was working with a client who told me that they could never upset the way things worked in their company. They couldn't tell their boss they felt there was a better way! This meant that they felt trapped in their career, incapable of achieving more and like they weren't meeting their true potential.

Enter frustration, anger, stress, work hatred and a sense of being trapped – if only they could get out of their comfort zone and tell their boss what they thought!

Learning to trust what they knew meant that they could rationalize and justify their thoughts and reasoning and work out what to do (if anything.)

We worked together to understand why they wanted to say something:

Was there envy at the boss's job or was this genuine belief that they knew a better way?

Could they prove what they felt was possible and the benefits to those involved?

Did they have ulterior motives that weren't positive?

What would be the best way to move forward and why would it work best for them?

If you need to learn to listen to yourself, start by asking questions (not looking for solutions) and you will start to ask some really smart questions that help you analyse your feelings, actions, etc without guilt, stress and other negative emotions getting in the way.

This process also allows you to find answers personalized to you. In my experience, so often it's the silly little ideas that have the most power. Okay so Dumbo is not considered a superhero – but think back to Dumbo and his magic feather that enabled him to fly, was there any magic?

Nope, but there was a belief that the magic existed – this process helps you do that.

This process also enables you to know when your own thoughts are doing their best to keep you trapped. You can become your own Kryptonite telling yourself the most awful things (that are usually not even true!) So be cautious of what you say to yourself and the questioning will help you to become more aware of this.

Choose your network wisely

We've all trusted someone and later questioned "How could I have let that person have had an impact on my life, thoughts and actions?"

Back to weird being a good thing, right?

But the fact is the people you choose to spend your time with can in their selves become a powerful tool to getting out of your comfort zone – but could also trap you there!

So, look out for the heroes in your life, that say things like:

"What's your thoughts on that? Do you think it's a good idea?"

"Where did your desire to do this come from?"

"Do you really want that or are you hiding something from yourself?

"Hang on a minute, you can do this, remember the time you did xxxx"

People that can supply you with evidence of your brilliance and who reinforce the positive and your goals, but also challenge your beliefs, thoughts and actions are like gold dust (or superhero serum.)

They will enable you to be able to take a step back and really understand why your comfort zones are controlling your life. They are there to celebrate your wins, appreciate your frustrations when it doesn't go to plan and give you the faith and confidence to keep going – don't think you can do it all on your own.

Everyone, even superheroes get an element of confidence from their network. It's not all internal!

And look out for the super villains who say:

"Are you sure you want to do that?"

"That sounds like a lot of work, are you up to that?"

"Why would you want to do that, I thought you loved your life/work/partner/house plant."

"You should tell them what you really think."

People that make comments like these aren't looking at it from your point of view, or with your ultimate wants and needs at the heart of their responses. They are seeing it from their perspective of life and their own limitations on what they feel can be achieved; and this influences the way they respond.

Yes, there are a few social vampires out there that will try and ruin your belief in anything better but, most super villains are far subtler than that.

3. GO DEEPER

In life, we often get an inkling of what needs to change or feel like something is not right. If you dig deeper, you usually find it's not the first thoughts that were the issue.

When I work with clients, the "Go deeper" exercise always (and I genuinely mean always!) produces the big Eureka moments. It's almost as if they are hearing their own voice for the first time.

Here's how to do it:

Firstly, start with a thought (any thought related to why you feel like there is a comfort zone or a fear) and write it down.

Now write below it the answer to this question: "And that means?"

Now below that ask yourself: "What does that mean?"

Keep going asking further questions like:

"So how does that affect me?"

"What does that mean to me?"

"Is that really what I think?"

"If this is the case what does that mean I must believe?

Does that serve me well?"

What does that mean?"

This process enables you to really explore what's going on in your brain and can be used in so many elements in your life.

4. BE YOUR OWN COACH

I've worked with coaches and mentors for many years and I don't think I could be without one to challenge me in the ways I've shared with you.

After years of challenging questions and realities, creating goals and getting great results, I know to a degree I can coach myself. As one coach told me "Mandie, you don't need anyone to kick your butt – you do it for yourself" That was a good session.

So sometimes, it's enough to coach yourself. By taking on the role of your own coach, just give yourself a little time once a month where you actually challenge what you think.

Here's a few ideas to help make that a powerful moment:

Free write

Don't think about what you write, just let the pen go to the paper and write anything – in the random thinking there is often the right questions and thoughts to follow – if you create the space to do it.

If you crave order and structure, don't free flow.

If you love art, then draw. If you hate numbers and lists, steer clear of them. You want to create a new way of thinking that is natural to you, not what you read in a book or heard in the office as "a good idea."

Learn to explore your natural style. Ask yourself: When set a task, how do I love to work, think, explore, learn, and act? This will guide you to the best approach to coaching yourself.

Create your own discipline

Do you need to diary time to be your own coach or is it enough to know that you want to do this and get results? Just like finding your natural style, you need to learn how you will create your own definition of discipline.

Get this wrong and you're highly unlikely to be taking action in 3 months' time!

Tell someone

I've seen some awesome planners laid out in many colours with lots of tabs and tons of ideas. But as that new client realized, great ideas are little use without action.

The first step to the action is to actually tell someone you are going to do it. Do you need to declare your goal online? Phone a friend or just stick a picture on your kitchen wall?

You will learn what makes you take action, which leads to our last idea...

5. KNOW WHEN TO START AND STOP

Knowing what to do and actually taking action and knowing when to stop and when to go for it are 2 especially important skills.

If you take action on what we talked about today, you will not only challenge yourself, but also challenge those that can manipulate and mould you.

You will learn to trust and have faith. Little by little (not always – some clients see massive levels of change after just a couple of hours), you will step out of your comfort zone. As I described it to one client years ago:

"Some people like to slowly step out of their comfort zones and others like to leap so far out that they can't see it any more. Learn to know which you are."

Neither is wrong, neither is right. Some people like big challenges, big goals, and big actions; others like no one to know what they aim to challenge but quietly work through their action plan to achieve it.

The true superhero in any film learns to know what works for them, accept it, love and go for it. And they don't need a scientist, a tycoon, or super villains either. Let me know how you get on.

20 LIFE COPING SKILLS THAT WILL HELP YOU STAY STRONG

Few things in life are guaranteed, although I can be quite certain when I say:

Someone is going to really annoy you.

Someone is going to die and leave you feeling empty and unable to go on. Something out of the blue is going to challenge you to the core of your humanity. Something is going to breakdown and stop working at the most inopportune moment you could imagine.

You are going to spend money on something you really don't want to.

You are going to be forced to do something you never thought you'd do.

You are going to face a challenge that feels completely soul des-troying...

How can you know these things, Mandie?

I hear you ask.

Well because as my dear Nan used to say, "In every life, a little rain must fall." Looking back as I watched Nan cook a meal worthy of gods or any childhood dream sequence, I know I used to struggle with what that saying meant.

Of course, some rain must fall, we would die without water, I used to think.

However, on the other side of childhood where bills, maintenance, insurance, and other boring things exist, I'm pretty sure I get the true meaning of that saying.

The intriguing thing is that I'm a keen reader and find that so much in personal and professional development and in the pursuit of happiness is aimed at ensuring we don't just have wellies, brollies and waterproofs, to protect us from the rain in life, but that we are so far removed from any wet stuff we can't appreciate the damage that this polar opposite can also have on our positive existence.

I want to share with you some of the top coping skills for life that aren't just good for the rainy days, they can have a serious impact on your life.

Into every life, some tough times appear, it is not the tough times that define us, it's how we deal with them that does.

All very well having great sentiments like that; however when your car has broken down, you feel ill and can't stop because deadlines are looming, your cat's puked in your shoes, your phone won't hold a charge, and they are making people redundant at work it can be hard to have the a positive "Can do" attitude.

Let's look at what to do (And I promise to make these ideas easy to action, life changing if applied, fast and reliable. Promise):

1. FIND OUT THE REAL CAUSE OF THE PROBLEM

I'm a keen believer that if you can't see what's going on, I mean really see, then you can't fix it. I'm often coaching a client who will walk in telling me that X is the issue when 20 minutes later we've delved into their minds and discovered that X was just a symptom of the problem.

And as you probably know treating symptoms and not the actual problem rarely works. The real issue is left to carry on wrecking your health, happiness and mental wellbeing.

How does this apply in stressful situations?

Have you ever had a friend that was pregnant, or you lost or gained weight, or realized that you were "suddenly" in this really bad habit of walking in the door at night and instantly grabbing a cold beverage?

That didn't just start, over time that gradually became more prominent. And when things sneak into our lives, be a beautiful baby bump or an unwanted 10lb, it didn't just land on you over-night.

2. ASK YOURSELF THE DIFFICULT QUESTIONS

So to find out how you are coping with stressful situations, ask yourself some questions:

How do I feel right now on a scale of 1 to 10? (10 being awesome and 1 being awful)

Is there a pattern to the way I feel caused by my environment?

Is there a pattern to the way I feel caused by my beliefs?

Is there a pattern to the way I feel caused by my work?

Take the time to process your response to these 4 questions. They could become powerful in every aspect of your life.

3. NOTICE YOUR REACTIONS

When we become aware of our surroundings, our situation, and the way they make us feel we need to learn to notice the impact of these things.

Not to start moaning at ourselves and berating us for being lazy, thick, stupid, sloppy, etc, just to notice. Above all it is about noticing the patterns we create, and this skill is about noticing how it impacts on you.

How does it make you feel?

How does it make you act?

How does it make you behave?

How does it make you think?

At this stage you don't have to think, do, say, or act any differently just notice what happens in stressful situations.

4. MEASURE AND LOCATE WHERE YOU ARE NOW

Peter Drucker famously says,[1]

"If you can't measure it, you can't improve it."

Therefore when you start to notice how you feel, act and behave in stressful times and have understood more about the way it impacts on you, you are then in a position to create a benchmark graph.[See below]

BENCH MARK GRAPH

As your coach I will help you achieve great things, overcome fear, rocket confidence and work towards what you want in life.
First we need to know where you are;

1. Use the bench mark graph to track how things are now.

2. In each circle write something that matters to you or that is impacting on success/work/life.

3. For each circle mark a cross of where you are now.

10 = awesome. 0 = awful.

2. Revisit this graph to assess how things are changing.

3. Revisit this graph at the end of our agreed goal achieving time to assess results.

4. How will you celebrate?

5. What needs to change/happen now?

(Suggestions for inclusion; Work, family, partner, finances, fun, respect, health, happiness)

WWW.MANDIEHOLGATE.CO.UK
COPYRIGHT 2018

5. BE HONEST ABOUT YOUR PROGRESS

In stressful situations, we can find ourselves with our heads down in the proverbial sand, with our hands over our ears yelling "la, la, la, la, la".

While as kids, that's hilarious to watch kids do that, as we grow up it's a bit of an ice-cold slap in the face that not being honest doesn't fix anything and stops us from changing things. Be honest as you create the above benchmark graph.

Being honest is a powerful thing. When you're honest with yourself, you raise self-awareness and anyone looking to achieve anything in the 21st century is going to be determined to improve their own self-awareness as we are starting to appreciate the power this can have.

Although Tasha Eurich[3] shares some scary research on this. Tasha Eurich, author of Insight; Why we've not as self-aware as we think and how seeing ourselves clearly helps us succeed at work and in life says in an interview for Harvard Business Review that "95% of people believe they're self-aware, however only about 10-15% actually are." Adding "The joke I always make is that on a good day, 80% of us are lying to ourselves about whether we're lying to ourselves." [4]

6. BE HONEST TO YOUR WORLD

In stressful times, it is not just important to be honest to ourselves, it's important that you're honest to those that are in your world. Some find that they can do this in their personal life but wouldn't dream of saying anything at work; whereas others bottle it all up, with a smile and a lie that says, "I'm fine."

7. IF YOU AREN'T FINE, SAY IT

You don't have to turn into a moaning black cloud of doom but being honest helps you and other people.

Showcasing your own limitations and stress can help other people to see the human that you are. We feel more connected to those that share honestly and are more likely to want to help them and at the very least probably less likely to add more to your workload.

I worked with someone that was petrified that work would find out how much they were struggling with the workload. This is what the conversation went like (and I'm sharing it so you can ask yourself similar questions):

Client: "I'm really struggling to hold it together."

Me: "Have you told anyone?"

Client: "I can't do that; it would be professional suicide. They'd be circling around me ready to pick the bones of my career in seconds."

Me: "Do you know that to be true?"

Client: "It's not worth the risk to find out."

Me: "So if you don't say something, what are you agreeing to?"

Client: "Feeling overwhelmed, stressed and about ready to quit."

Me: "And are you happy to stay there or would you like to be somewhere else?"

Client: "Obviously somewhere else, but I can't see how that's possible.

Me: "Are you prepared to explore where you would like to be and how to get there?"

You can guess the answer! And using the tools below, guess what they discovered?

They weren't alone! It was an issue throughout the department and changes were made for everyone. A bit of honesty can go along way! And yes, I know that can be scary do to.

8. TAKE ACTIONS TO CHANGE

In stressful situations, the human being is pre-programmed to do everything in its power to escape the situation it finds itself in.

Fight or flight doesn't really do this pre-programming justice. We are still alive because since the dawn of our time we've been able to adapt, change and escape situations that other species succumb to.

The issue is that we also fear change. I get more speaking engagements and corporate coaching gigs because people are struggling with change than possibly any other subject. The fact is while we can appreciate change can help in stressful situations, knowing and doing is not the same thing.

Ask yourself what could I change about this situation? (This is not what am I going to do, this is about making suggestions about what you could do.) And if they are the suggestions that have been rattling around in your head for the last few weeks, or keep you awake at night, they are less likely to be useful.

Really get in touch with your subconscious (and the good ideas) by asking:

"If money, time, skill, health, magic, beliefs or values weren't factors in this situation what could I do?"

This enables your mind to explore some whacky ideas, however as Einstein (may have said) Creativity is intelligence having fun. And this exercise enables your mind to have some fun.

9. DON'T CHANGE WHAT YOU CAN'T CHANGE

I worked with a large organization that had been through massive change. Everyone had stepped up to the challenge, but everyone was really stressed. Those that were struggling the most kept reminding me that "it hadn't always been like this", and "the old way was a lot easier".

Not all change can be controlled. And when we fight it, we can find ourselves escalating stress. Sometimes the most powerful thing you can do is learn to go with the flow.

If you don't "choose" to go with the flow, ask yourself:

What are you agreeing to?

This question enables you to see that you are going to get negative emotions, actions, conversations, damaged relationships and even health issues.

Change is sometimes dumped on us like a storm clouds contents, you could stand and moan at the storm cloud, but it won't stop you from getting wet.

10. ASK YOURSELF: ARE YOU CREATING IT?

Some of life's stresses are man-made. And I'm not talking about someone else, I'm talking about you.

It is an ugly fact that none of us want to look at (so be brave) however have the strength to ask, "Am I creating this stress?"

Remember to be honest. And let the answers come to you.

11. KNOW THAT SH*T HAPPENS

First spotted in the 60's, this has been a famous saying since at least the 80's, why? Because stuff does just happen.

As humans we are always looking for reason and understanding. "Why did this happen to me?" and we can often find ourselves down a rabbit run looking for ghosts of answers that just don't exist.

Sometimes bad stuff happens. This does not define you. This is not a personal vendetta from a god or unseen deity, seriously sometimes all you can do is accept those 2 words – sh*t happens.

12. CONTROL
YOUR MINDSET

A quick way to find yourself suffering an intenser version of stress is when you try to control it.

As a coach, I believe we can get out of situations and move forward, however I also know from the coping skill above that when we try to force the universe to bend in a new way, it can use up a lot of energy concentrating on the wrong things.

You can control what you think, you can change your actions, and sometimes the most powerful skill is to accept that this is out of your hands. Self-awareness will help you understand the differences and what to do and when.

13. SAY NO MORE OFTEN

We talked about the need to be honest and if you explore this coping mechanism further, you will see that as humans we really want to be liked. We want to get on with our neighbours, or colleagues our friend's friends. The issue with this in stressful times we really do need to turn around and say things like:

No sorry I can't help you.

No, now is not a good time.

No, I'm not finding this easy.

No, I can't do it.

The reason we don't say things like this is because we fear what people think of us. We want to be liked. We don't want people think we don't care, which leads me onto the next point.

14. EMBRACE WEAKNESS

The above statements are often held in our heads unsaid because we don't want to appear weak, awkward, incapable and a ton of other negatives. The interesting thing is that what we think people are thinking about us is so often untrue.

Take the client above that feared telling their boss they were struggling with their workload. On the contrary to looking weak and incapable, the whole department got a makeover. That's not weak, that's powerful.

Watch out for the incorrect falsehoods that you let hang out in your head. They are making stressful situations a lot harder!

The next time it feels weak to be honest or to say no, ask yourself "Does the way I currently think serve me well?"

15. SET CLEAR BOUNDARIES

Boundaries are important to us all. It feels great when we get on holiday and we can do what we like when we like, however left like that for more than a few weeks and things can disintegrate and fall apart.

We need boundaries. And at stressful times, boundaries can really help. They enable you to feel safe to be honest and work and think in a way that helps you and they set out what you will tolerate and deal with and what you won't.

Remember creating boundaries is a lot like saying no and most of the negative thoughts you are having around boundaries are imaginary too. If you aren't going to answer work email at 10pm on a Saturday night, don't.

Establish your boundaries, communicate them, and stick by them.

16. GET PASSIONATE ABOUT SOMETHING

In stressful times, we can find ourselves living in negative, soul destroying emotions and moods. To the point that we can attempt to numb ourselves from them.

The next time the emotions start to impact on you, think about all the things that you are passionate about.

No one need know what you are thinking about, so if you find yourself thinking about your dog before your partner, that's fine.

Get yourself a big old list that makes you smile. Even if the smile doesn't feel real, your brain is still benefiting. When we get really bogged down in stressful times, it can be hard to believe that we will ever feel good again.

We can't change everything instantly but interestingly (and I find miraculously), we can change our mindset in the click of a finger. Getting passionate could help you do that.

17. ASK FOR WHAT YOU TRULY WANT

If you need time, a hug, a conversation, a massage, a run, a nap, a walk, a helping hand, ask for it.

Of all the fears in my book Fight the Fear, so many come back to the fear of what other people will think of us and I've heard so many people tell me that they've learnt to ask for what they want.

Stop fearing asking for what you need. Learn to accept that asking for what you want not only helps you navigate through stressful times; it also helps you to achieve more in life too.

18. DITCH THE GUILT

Guilt just loves tough times. It will be able to give you a voice in your head that tells you:

This is all your fault.

You never get it right.

You've always failed at this.

You should have taken better care of that.

You weren't good enough to get that job.

If someone had to go, it had to be you.

No one sticks around you for long.

This is you, what were you expecting?

That voice is worse than Cruella Deville, Voldemort and Hannibal Lector combined. It's intent on destroying your determination and happiness.

Have you noticed how some people go through hell and keep going and others suffer far less and give up? The reason they keep going is not some shot of good fortune, it comes down to what they let happen in their head. So, chuck the guilt.

19. NEVER HATE STRESS

It's no good hating stressful times, it won't make them magically disappear.

Stress is an essential component to your body. Without some stress between bones, muscles, skin, etc you would be a floppy mess on the floor.

Stress can help us grow and learn so much about ourselves. What could you discover about you from the stress you face right now? And don't just look for the negative, there is some good in there, so keep looking!

20. START MOVING

When life feels too tough, we can be tempted to hide our heads under the duvet and say "give me a call in 2050, I will come out when its all over"

Trust me, I include myself in that one.

In my personal life, I've seen a lot of awful things. Don't try and be superhuman, as I read in The Last Highlander, when you face the most horrific of times, just concentrate on getting one foot in front of the other.

GO THE EXTRA MILE

In stressful times we need people around us that will go the extra mile, and I'm one of those.

Watch out for the sappers of positivity and remember the basics – sleep, eat, breathe – get those in the right measures especially when you are struggling, you see as Nan so wisely knew we can't hide from tough times, we can't make them magically disappear, however like a storm cloud it will eventually go away.

And behind it is left that fresh new smell that says, "Mmm anything is possible"

And do you know what?

It is.

[1]   ^   Drucker Institute:
www.drucker.institute/perspective/about-peter-drucker/

[2]   ^   Mandie Holgate: Bench Mark Graph
www.mandieholgate.co.uk/bench-mark-graph-where-am-i/

[3]   ^   Tasha Eurich: www.tashaeurich.com

[4]   ^   Harvard Business Review:
https://hbr.org/2018/01/what-self-awareness-really-is-and-how-to-cultivate-it

WHAT NOW?

If you have taken the time to read and action every chapter with every tool, technique, and strategy you should be seeing changes in your life. If you aren't, be honest with yourself.

Take a few moments to write down what you are thinking.

Are you holding on to beliefs that say "this stuff could never work for me because...?"

Or are you thinking something else?

Find the automatic way of thinking that is whirling around in your head telling you that change is not possible and that you can't have better results.

Challenge what you hear and see which chapters resonate with you most and revisit them.

We are all beautifully unique and yet we all need to power up the quality of our minds to get what we want out of life.

You can do this too. I believe in you.

I love hearing from readers so do feel free to get in touch. Years on I still get messages and pictures from people around the world who have read *Fight the fear – how to beat your negative mindset and win in life* sharing their life changing moments and Eureka's.

You can access all of my social media accounts via my website – www.mandieholgate.co.uk or email me at mandie@mandieholgate.co.uk

I also have courses, books and a confidential mastermind group through my organisation www.thebusinesswomansnetwork.co.uk and I share free content on my website.

If you would like to know more about coaching in your workplace or on a one to one basis getting to know me through social media will help you decide if I'm right for you and I'm happy to have a chat anytime.

To sign up to my newsletter head to my site and then you can be the first to hear of new books, courses, speaking engagements and articles to power up your mind and take control.

I've always believed that everyone is capable of achieving everything they really want to and through my work I aim to prove it. You deserve the happiness and success you want so let's keep in touch and make it a reality.